Common Worship in Church Schools

An Experiment in Integration

Ian Dewar

Vicar of All Saints, App'~~ ~~·'

GROVE BOOKS LIMITED
RIDLEY HALL RD CAMBRIDGE CB3 9HU

Contents

Acknowledgments

The author is grateful to Miss Jane Phythian, Headteacher, Miss Nicola Hill and pupils of year 3 and year 4, Mrs Dawn Glover and pupils of year 4 and year 5 at All Saints CE Primary School for their help and enthusiasm in this experiment.

The Cover Illustration is by Peter Ashton

First Impression February 2003
ISSN 0144-1728
ISBN 1 85174 522 X

Introduction 1

The General Synod of the Church of England has decided that Church schools are central to its mission.

Whether we are in agreement with this idea or not it is clear that resources and energy are being directed to this area of church life. At the same time as huge changes and developments have been taking place in the world of education (not just Church schools) the Church of England has been completely revising its liturgy. Coincidence? No! Whilst changes in education have been politically led, and much of the work relating to Church schools has been in response to this, there is a more fundamental or structural shift taking place.

21st century Britain may not be post-religious, but in many ways it is post-Christian. The Church of England, liturgically, pastorally, structurally and in education is having to adjust to a world that did not exist 50 years ago.

We are faced with a dilemma. An historical faith must incarnate itself in a postmodern culture. And a major opportunity for this exists where a proper conversation takes place between *Common Worship* and the world of education. Sadly, I am not persuaded that this conversation is taking place at the level it ought to.

This booklet is aimed at all—clergy or lay—who are involved in the leading of worship in Church schools. Its primary contention is that there is a level of confusion in the world of education about *Common Worship*. However, this is not just related to the introduction of new liturgical material. I have had contact with Church schools since 1992 and have noticed that as far as liturgical worship is

An historical faith must incarnate itself in a postmodern culture

concerned, church and school have been operating on very different principles. Whilst there are legitimate reasons for this there must come a point where a consensus of opinion is reached so that both church and school can reflect the life of a worshipping community. This booklet will look at how we have tried to achieve this in our particular parish. It is my hope that you will be able to extract principles and practices that can be applied to your own situation and use them for developing your own local practices within the framework and ethos of *Common Worship*.

To do this we need to ask why the split between church and school has occurred. By using the word 'split' I am not implying that there was necessarily any common liturgical practice in the past. What I have in mind is the cultural shift emphasized by Callum Brown who states, 'Religion mattered and mattered deeply in British society in the 1950s. But it started to stop mattering in the 1960s.'[1] The 'British people re-imagined themselves in ways no longer Christian.'[2] Pinning this down liturgically it seems to me that there are three key elements.

1 The world of education does exactly what it claims—it educates. The education of pupils is so ingrained in staff that worship largely becomes a matter of education. However, worship is more than just education and the question can be fairly asked, how many teachers are 'trained' or 'experienced' worship leaders? The requirement to deliver daily acts of collective worship in a time-pressured environment encourages those leading worship to instinctively rely on skills they are confident with—teaching. Thus a Bible story can easily become 'a moral story' rather than an encounter with God.

2 Recent years have seen a considerable shift in liturgical thinking. In the past liturgy was the book; now it is shape and structure. A driving force behind this has been the growing sense that the church has to rediscover its roots. As far as liturgical development is concerned the question must be put, to what extent have liturgists seen schools as an intrinsic part of the roots and life of the church? Like teachers, liturgists do what liturgists do and unless they have children I suspect few give the world of education serious thought.

3 The major impact on worship in the post-war period must surely be the Charismatic Movement; 'the last few decades of the twentieth century have brought a totally new experience of worship.'[3] It has given rise to widespread use of worship songs, music groups and an emphasis on 'free' (not book-bound) worship. This model fits perfectly for young children and given the post-war thinking in education that learning starts where the child is—not book bound or 'given'—it is not hard to see why this style of worship, song, talk, prayers, is easily transferable into a school setting. The potentially negative impact of this kind of worship in church life is recognized in *Patterns for Worship*. 'Both structure and contents are so free and variable that people see no links with traditional Anglican worship' (Introduction, p 3). What is practised in school will often not match what is practised in church, thereby deepening the alienation between the worship of the local church and the worship experiences of the children in school.

A Way Forward

2

Is there a way in which the worlds of education and liturgy can be reconciled?

To begin answering this question we need to establish some clear parameters.

1   Children come to school for an education not to worship. It is a different 'primary' reason for attendance than for those who go to church. Clearly any self-respecting Church school will contain in its prospectus words to the effect 'The religious education and worship provided by the school is in accordance with the Church of England foundation...removal of pupils from Religious Education or acts of Collective Worship cannot insulate pupils from the religious life of the school.' This option, however, highlights the point that parents will often choose a school for a variety of reasons other than the fact it is part of a worshipping community.

2   There is the issue of culture—how does living in a postmodern world affect Church schools and *Common Worship*? Canon John Hall, General Secretary of the National Society, pointed out to me that there does not appear to be any major research into what values shape a postmodern child. Two crucial questions seem to be, what is the impact on the mental, moral and spiritual outlook of children born into a postmodern culture and does Church school worship provide children with the necessary equipment to legitimately question and challenge that world?[4] Speaking liturgically and (by implication) missiologically we have not yet begun to wrestle with the whole area of cultural values and child development. As one youth worker puts it, 'In our enthusiasm to explain that Jesus is the answer, we overlook the fact that nobody is asking the question.'[5] The implicit values 'brought' into schools by the young are often radically different from the gospel's. (This seems to me especially true in aspirant socio-economic areas.) Worship and liturgical formation may be the sharp point of conflict/meeting between these different world views.

3   Spirituality is on the agenda. For how long is anybody's guess and its depth and quality are open to question. Nonetheless it is a window of opportunity. We can talk unashamedly of the 'Other' or the 'spiritual life.'

4   Parents expect there to be something different about a Church school. This tends to be in terms of morality and standards of behaviour. Whether they see this as a partnership with themselves, a supplement for perceived common values or as a substitute for areas they find difficult (as with Sex Education) I do not know. It is probably a mixture of all three with the latter two dominant.

The role of worship in this matrix of attitudes takes effect on two levels. First, it simply happens. Parents do have the right to withdraw their child(ren) from collective worship but my impression is that this right is rarely exercised. Even (perhaps especially) in Church schools with a large or majority ethnic minority intake it is taken as *prima facie* that worship will happen. This is the context in which school worship must be shaped and given substance. The major strength of *Common Worship* here is that it makes a principle of allowing different building blocks to create different emphases in worship that can both reflect and challenge local culture.

Secondly, there is its 'quality.' This is the cutting edge of school worship because here shape, structure and content will start to have an impact. School worship becomes a cup into which can be poured all the innocent energies, hopes, fears, and aspirations of the children. At the same time it becomes a point of dialogue. The shape and content of school worship will give rise to questions in children's minds suggested by the material chosen—readings, hymns, prayers and greetings. These questions can crystallize the conversation that takes place (or needs to take place) between the gospel and the wider culture. So, for example, affirming children as being made in the image of God is easy in some areas ('My child is special') hard in others, ('If I am special why do my parents hit me?') though always open to misunderstanding ('my special child doesn't sin' and, 'I must have been bad and God is punishing me.')[6]

It is the task of the Holy Spirit to conver or affirm what is already in existence

The quality, emphases and patterns of worship in a Church school have to deal with the 'givens' of the faith and root them within the locality in which the school operates. This is hard work which demands a great deal of soul searching on the part of the governors and the local church as to what is mission of the church in that locality.

The question can be raised as to whether or not school worship is proselytizing or affirming natural spirituality. I do not think that either of these is a legitimate option. It is the task of the Holy Spirit to convert or affirm what is already in existence. The task of the school/church partnership is to work to create the conditions in which the work of the Holy Spirit may best be facilitated.

Our Pattern of Worship

We now need some practical examples. The guiding principle behind what we are trying to achieve at All Saints (church and school) is that of liturgical formation. We have begun to establish a pattern of worship which links church and school together. The broad brush is as follows.

First, there is the midweek service in church on Thursdays at 9.15am to which the school comes but it is open to all. When the service has finished for the children there is a short break. After this break the service continues with Holy Communion and any adults who wish to stay for this are welcome to do so. We realize that for many people Sunday can be a day of catching up with the family and so we are trying to provide an opportunity for people to receive communion. *Secondly*, there is a new service that takes place on the third Sunday of each month. This non-Communion service is based on the first part of the structure of the Service of the Word with Holy Communion found in the new *Common Worship* material. It lasts approximately 40 minutes and is similar to Thursday mornings. The important thing is that pupils begin to know parts of the service off by heart and this is now being developed to include chants. The parts that they learn are used on Thursdays, the third Sundays and on the other Sundays which are full Communion services. This is really important because it means that at each service any pupil (or parent) who comes along will find something familiar and be able to follow the worship more easily.

3

Form of Service at All Saints Primary, Appley Bridge

(Thursday Morning—Ordinary Time)

Grace, mercy and peace from God our Father
and the Lord Jesus Christ be with you.
And also with you.

Lord, direct our thoughts, teach us to pray,
lift up our hearts to worship you in Spirit and in truth,
through Jesus Christ. **Amen.**

God our Father, we come to you in sorrow for our sins.

For the mean thoughts we have had, Father forgive us: **and help us.**

For the hurtful words we have said, Father forgive us: **and help us.**

For the wrong things we have done, Father forgive us: **and help us.**

Reading *(Read by a pupil)*

Talk

Hymn or Creed

Prayers *(Led by pupils who are invited to submit topics for prayer)*

(We pray for God's grace, saying:
Lord, receive our praise **and hear our prayer.**)

Lord God, through your grace we are your people;
through your Son you have redeemed us;
in your Spirit you have made us as your own.

The full text of the intercessions can be found in Patterns for Worship
(original) p 88

Lord's Prayer

(Certificates, birthdays and so on)

The peace of the Lord be always with you. **And also with you.**
(The peace is shared between pupils, staff and parents)

Go in peace to love and serve the Lord. **In the name of Christ.**

Seasonal Material for Advent

Introduction

> **Soloist** 1 verse from O come, O come, Emmanuel
> **All** **Rejoice, rejoice! Emmanuel**
> **shall come to thee, O Israel.**
> *(During this the Advent candle is lit by a child from the Early Years)*

Intercessions

In joyful expectation of his coming we pray to Jesus, saying,
Maranatha. **Come, Lord Jesus.**

The full text of the intercessions can be found in Patterns for Worship
(original) p 66

Both Services then continue with the Liturgy of the Sacrament

Commentary

Time is marked out into **seasons** and this is reflected both in the text (with a seasonal liturgical greeting), in church (with the appropriate liturgical colours) and in school hymn practice where special or appropriate material is learnt and explained.

The service begins with a **liturgical greeting**. This teaches that we gather *together* for worship. It is where we move from everyday cordiality, 'Good morning everyone,' to divine cordiality, 'Grace, mercy and peace…'

Confession is a simplified form adapted from Patterns for Worship but maintaining a classic Anglican threefold confession of thought, word and deed. Silence is used to give worshippers time to wrestle with the issues and help set a prayerful atmosphere for what is taking place. Whilst it is not taken directly from authorized texts it seeks to remain faithful to the intention of Anglican worship. It is intended from the outset that all worship should be: 'prayerful, confident, generous, corporate, leisurely.'[7]

The public **reading of Holy Scripture** by pupils indicates the importance of being shaped by the

With the liturgical greeting we move from everyday cordiality to divine cordiality

9

Bible. As parents are present it is precisely that, a *public* reading. Following discussions with staff at the school we have sought to devise a school lectionary based on the main Sunday Gospel reading. This is discussed in chapter six.

The talk is a wonderful opportunity to be creative. It can be a simple object talk, question and answer, role play by pupils (and occasionally parents) or a mixture of these or other styles.

Prayer is led by pupils from year 6. We have initially settled on this age group because these children are mature enough to begin this process and the leaving of this role to Y6 pupils gives something for others to aspire to. Training is important and time is spent with pupils talking about placing prayer requests in appropriate categories—the World, the Church, the Sick—and using language to vocalize them properly.

Prayer allows children to make connections between their growing experience of life and Christian faith

Prayer allows children to begin exploring what are often thought of as adult themes and to make connections between their growing experiences of life and Christian faith. Jesus of course tells us that to enter the kingdom of heaven we must become like little children (Mark 10.14). However, he does not tell us to stop there and in the epistle to the Hebrews we are expressly told to 'move on' from spiritual milk (Hebrews 6.1).

The prayers end with the Lord's Prayer which is also used at the end of the Eucharistic Prayer. This is a slight variation on the Service for Holy Communion in the *Prayer Book* which starts with the Lord's Prayer and also repeats it after consecration and reception.

Song is a much neglected area in common debate. What is the role of song or hymnody in Christian formation? John Bell from the Iona Community argued at the Blackburn Diocesan Conference, that song is culture-forming.[8] The way to do this with schools is to get someone from the local church (not necessarily the vicar) to attend the school's hymn practice so that material can be explained and a non-verbal message communicated that this is important.

The Peace feels a bit like the Byzantine rite (in Greek or Russian) which still contains the words for the dismissal of the catechumenate (those preparing for baptism). Its importance is that it teaches the children to use their bodies a bit more in worship and allows them to shake hands with a teacher which is both adult and reinforces the concept of this being a 'common' act. The children leave at this point (unless it is a Feast Day in which case year 6 stay.)

Some comment needs to be made as to why, if the children are dismissed, we have Communion. There are three simple reasons for this.

(a) It plants in the children's minds the idea that something else important can and does take place. It arouses their curiosity.

(b) It provides for the church a midweek Eucharist where adults who no longer have primary aged children can worship with the school.

(c) It encourages parents who do not attend on Sundays to stay and builds a practice for them to worship regularly.

There is a question about the age at which children are confirmed and admitted to Holy Communion. Practice is so varied in this area that each parish must decide its own course of action.

Worship in the Seasons

This is similar in format to Ordinary Time except that it clearly has seasonal material. There are only two comments to make here.

In our culture the **lighting of candles** is generally perceived to be a 'religious' or 'spiritual' act (often related to an expression of grief). Its use in church in this particular setting and with this liturgy gives the lighting of candles in the Advent wreath a context by which to define their meaning. Thus a candle is not simply a sign of hope—it is a sign of hope focused on the coming of Christ into the world, as a baby who will grow into a man and embrace death and resurrection. The candle is lit by a child whilst the rest of the school sings a verse of 'O come, O come Emmanuel.'

The use of the **Maranatha litany** provides a spiritual, educational and cultural opportunity. It is spiritual, in that children are using the language of the first Christians—Aramaic—and are therefore tapping into the worship life of the church throughout the ages. It is educational because of the opportunity to discuss history and linguistics. It is cultural because it gently challenges the commonly held instinct of people for 'abandoning...all that was associated with the past.'[9]

There are a variety of spin-offs from this approach, such as turning the school nativity into an act of worship, but I will not overload you with these.

Does it Work?

The project has been in operation for over 12 months and its potential impact may not be known for a number of years. However, initial evidence is that it works. Pupils respond well to responsibility and are comfortable with structure and guidelines.

Particularly important has been the practice of pupils leaving at the Peace unless it is a Feast Day (such as Ascension) when Y6 pupils stay behind. Unless confirmed they do not communicate but at the end receive the 'blessed bread.' This is an idea taken from the Byzantine practice of the 'antidoron.'

In the Byzantine tradition there is still the practice of taking bread for Communion and separating it into two.[10] Part is for consecrating and part is for blessing and distributing to everyone at the end of the liturgy. (To some extent this reflects the fact that currently in the Byzantine tradition people do not receive communion weekly).

Its usefulness to us is that we have found an important half-way house of inclusiveness. Those who do not receive communion (mainly children) are conscious that there is a difference between the bread given with the chalice and the bread given out at the end of the liturgy. However, the use and distribution of bread in this way has led to a noticeable degree of togetherness as have other shared acts such as the children placing ashes on each other on Ash Wednesday.

How Do We Apply This to Church Life?

We have a major advantage at All Saints in that church and school are next door to each other. Where this is not the case worship leaders may need to try and transform the school hall or even place attendance at church once a half-term in the School Development Plan.[11]

Twice a year (with episcopal blessing) we move our main Sunday Communion service from church to school, using the structure of the school service. The change of venue has taught us a great deal about our worship. It allows us to contribute to the spirituality of our school by simply carrying out such an act. It has also helped us to begin exploring the potential for having a Communion service in school when parents are present, as at an end of term event.

Principles of liturgical structure and shape are taken seriously in both contexts and become interchangeable

I have already mentioned above that on the third Sunday in the month we have a Service of the Word which extends the structure and principles of the Thursday school worship. What we are therefore doing is creating a common body of material for church and school. Principles of liturgical structure and shape are taken seriously in both contexts and become interchangeable. Liturgical behaviour is also learnt in a common fashion. To know when to stand, to sit, to kneel, to learn different postures of prayer, all helps to take away the 'fear' of what is 'right' in church.

This crossover or continuum of worship between church and school can allow children to play. The Archbishop of Canterbury, Rowan Williams, has written of children that, 'to learn language is to discover, by trial and error, what I can seriously be committed to when I open my mouth.'[12] By using 'strange' and 'unusual' formularies of words, children are legitimately playing at expressing the inexpressible. 'Can you find out the deep things of God?' (Job 11.7).

Moreover, acting out and dealing with some of life's key dramas—birth, marriage and death—is potentially a profound way of giving children safe space to meet life's key issues. Baptizing baby dolls or action men, marrying giggling juniors or asking for volunteers to be a dead body are sure ways of engaging childrens' imaginations. If a school has the appropriate mechanism this may also lead to opportunities for children to speak to teachers about any pain or anxiety they have. Thus pastoral care can arise from good liturgical practice.

Pastoral care can arise from good liturgical practice

Conclusion

These are personal observations but I think they contain some important principles. A key feature of the future success of this development is education. For example, time needs to be made to go into school to teach pupils about prayer and how it can be led. What is prayer? Can you express pain in prayer? How are you supposed to talk to God? This requires serious wrestling by the local church on its use of resources and its overall vision of its mission. What I think is crucial is that many of the issues to be wrestled with in schools are the same as those to be wrestled with in churches, and that schools (more so than churches) are an intense focus of what we have to engage with in society as a whole.

The final point, however, is how far can we take this? Can these principles be adapted to class worship as well as whole school worship?

4   Class Worship—The Experiment

As it is important that those reading this booklet see exactly what we have attempted at All Saints, this chapter will simply detail the process followed for half a term with teacher observations. An assessment of the evidence will form the next chapter.

The class chosen was a mixed group of Y3 and Y4 pupils—lower juniors. This was done in consultation with the Headteacher. Space timetabled for the teaching of RE was allocated to me on two consecutive Monday afternoons. This space was used by working with the pupils on the story of St Columba journeying from Ireland to Scotland, establishing a community there and discussing how the monks would have had a rhythm of prayer. It was then explained to the pupils that they were going to be those monks for the next few weeks.

A major consideration in class worship is how to structure it and the following points were considered:

1 The shape of the room and its layout. What can and cannot be adjusted to change the atmosphere?

2 Posture of those present. Sitting, standing, kneeling?

3 Roles of worshippers. 5 key roles per act of worship:

    • leader
    • lighter of candles
    • reader
    • cantor
    • intercessor

    These roles can be rotated weekly, termly etc.

4 The shape of the liturgy.

    Greeting
    Opening prayer

Silence
Reading from Scripture (2–3 verses only, style is meditative)
Chant or canticle
Silence
Prayer (litany style, 3 responses only.)
Lord's Prayer
Dismissal

Time allowed—10 minutes.

For worship the teacher and I decided that it was best if the children stood in a semi-circle around the edge of the class carpet where story work takes place. The five roles were all allocated to the children. Below is the text itself, followed by my observations and comments by the class teacher.

Class Worship

(Mrs Hill Y3/Y4)

The room is prepared (tables and chairs moved)

Gather round the worship table in silence

Silence

Candle boy/girl lights the candle

The Lord is here. **His Spirit is with us.**

Lord Jesus we gather together to worship you.
You are our friend and our God.
May we know your love and your joy of life. **Amen.**

Reader

Cantor: Song

Prayer leader   Lord, receive our praise
All   **And hear our prayer.**

The Lord's Prayer

Go in peace to love and serve the Lord. **In the name of Christ. Amen.**

The candles are blown out in silence and children return to their seats

Worship 1

The act of worship took 10 minutes from arrival in the classroom to the end of the act itself and the actual worship about 7 minutes. This could be shorter or longer with practice on the use of time, silence and space. It is possible even on this first observation to notice that children will quickly be able to dispense with sheets and learn certain parts of the liturgy off by heart. There is a question of the lectionary—do we go for *lectio divina*[13] or larger continuous passages? It may well be that there is a place for both. The *lectio divina* approach would restrict the reading of Scripture to one or two verses. A continuous form, however, would allow for longer readings. In this case I would strongly recommend the avoidance of teaching type passages, such as epistles or monologues, and concentrate on, for example, four weeks of the adventures of David or what happened after Jesus was born (flight into Egypt). A simple structure might be: David is anointed; David kills Goliath; David is afraid; David meets death. This gives little snapshots of David's life which allows children to build stories in their own imaginations. There are also issues relating to the choice of volunteers. Throughout the school cycle all should have some degree of responsibility. There is also the issue of music, the quality of which must be built up.

Throughout the school cycle all should have some degree of responsibility

Teacher Comments

Children were attentive and organized if a little hesitant about their leadership roles, but this is just due to the fact that they need to get used to taking responsibility for themselves and not being afraid of showing leadership qualities amongst their peers. They enjoyed the worship and commented later on in the day 'When are we having the next one?' 'Is it every day?'

Worship 2

I have decided to go for *lectio divina*, four readings over the next four weeks based on the suggestion above about David. The teacher is to ask the pupils at the end of the day what they can remember from each verse.

This week the children (apart from those leading) did not use sheets and the new material felt comfortable. The volunteers seemed to be more relaxed and growing in confidence. Pupils joined the circle well to begin worship and silence improved in quality. The singing was much better than the previous week. The children still needed encouragement from the teacher but it was interesting to see how this actually progressed. In order to help with the intercessions I asked the children what they wanted to pray for. They said the obvious in terms of pets but then came a desire for a good day at school, someone's grandmother who was ill and somebody whose parents need to stop smoking—they were worried about their health. These were written on a board so the person leading the prayers could see them clearly.

Teacher Comments
Children were much better at organizing themselves as they were aware of what it required of them. They do not need the sheets as they already know the responses required. A number of children are starting to relate to this time as the quiet peaceful time for thinking and one child has stated 'It's a good start to the day Miss! It gets you ready and settled.' I asked the children after today's session how they felt about the new style of worship in class and all had positive responses.

Some mentioned that lighting the candle was calming and they enjoyed looking at the flames. Overall so far the response is very positive.

Worship 3

The children responded immediately when told worship was happening, there was no sense of confusion. The worship leader needs a little more encouragement at this stage to find her feet. The two pupils who lead the music made a suggestion of their own for a song to sing. It was, *He's Got The Whole World in His Hands*. The person responsible, Alistair, needed the minimum of prompting in order to lead the prayers. Topics for prayers were also interesting and out came two light ones and one serious one. The reading was read with some degree of relish, David killing Goliath, it is a good strong story and appeals to young minds. Overall all pupils seemed to be growing in confidence with the responses. They still need some leading and prompting but this is simply a case of classroom culture.

The children responded immediately when told worship was happening

Teacher Comments
A very organized session. It flowed without any problems. Children are starting to volunteer ideas for prayers and one child was very assertive as to the choice of hymn to be sung. The children are definitely involved in this service and are starting to see it as their own.

After questioning about the Bible reading the children remembered the following things: David killed Goliath with the stone; and he cut off his head using a sword (they could not remember whose sword it was).

Worship 4

The children were already sitting on the classroom mat when I arrived. Volunteers moved tables to create space. The children stood round in a circle. There was some sense of giddiness but it may just be that they anticipated and knew what was coming. I gave the person reading, Harriet, a verse to read from the Bible with two difficult words, 'dath' and 'adullam.' With a little prompting she handled the words very well. She is a Y4 child. The rest of the verse was read very smoothly. This may reflect ability but I think it also indicates familiarity of task and regularity of practice. Therefore, new things can be easily introduced within the security of a structure.

This time pupils were uncertain what to choose to sing. A couple of suggestions were made but these were beyond the ability of the group. In the end the pupils settled on *O Lord hear my prayer*. This was sung three times with good control and volume. This had been learnt in church worship two weeks ago and used in the Harvest service as an entrance piece. To help provide some partnership with the church it was also used on Sunday at the Harvest festival so children could make connections between the two.

They are relating their life experiences to the space provided in this worship to speak to God about them

The prayers chosen were again interesting. Again we had a hamster, this time dying. This provides an opportunity to deal with death and dying for children in a familiar setting. We had the issue of a pet being born. We also had the issues of families, one person in one family dying and in another a new baby being born. It appears children are getting confident about relating their life experiences to the space provided in this worship to speak to God about them. It is important to recognize here, I think, that if we take a hamster dying seriously that it sends a signal to the child that we also take the thoughts of their grandma dying seriously as well. It is a question of building trust.

There is possibly an issue to concentrate on here. It may be that children need two to three lessons on how to deliver material. This could be a fun exercise—how to project your voice, to breathe properly and of course would tie in nicely with health, spirituality (all major religions teach and speak of the importance of posture and breathing) and possibly the natural science of the human body.

At the end of worship I asked the children to recap on a story I had told them about St Columba over three weeks ago in RE. They did so very well.

The children are now in a routine and have started reminding the class teacher that it is worship this morning and telling the class teacher what they need to do. For example, 'Shall we move the tables? Is everybody ready on the mat?' The worship is flowing well and without interruption now. All children understand the need to participate.

Worship 5

It is now almost too easy to worship. When I walk into the classroom the children who are leading in certain roles get up and stand there ready waiting for their pieces of paper and the organization of the day's prayers. When I ask what we wish to pray for today hands shoot up immediately and a good number of suggestions come out. An interesting turn on this occasion was the introduction by the children of prayers of celebration. We were asked to pray for Oliver's birthday, that it would be a good and exciting day. This indicates a classroom community but also a recognition that we can pray not just about sad things but also about the joys of life.

This time the children chose a piece of music that was slightly more complicated than normal and needed singing in rounds. They did this with little help from the class teacher—very competently. Again familiarity with structure allows them to stretch and experiment with something new. It is perhaps also an indication of the confidence they are gaining in using this form of worship.

Teacher Comments
Children have started asking when we are changing the leaders' roles. Even some of the more shy children have requested to take an active part in the sessions. I think a new set of leaders after the half-term would be good and timed about right. The session flowed smoothly with the children wanting to perform more complicated versions of the song. Children are starting to look forward to the session.

5 Commentary on the Experiment

Undoubtedly life is made easier by willing and enthusiastic pupils but at this age you would be hard pushed to find pupils who did not have some element of willingness or enthusiasm.

There now follows a list of principles that I have taken from the experiment that can be used to adapt it to other school settings.

Avoid A Siege Mentality
It is very easy for clergy and other leaders of school worship to perceive it to be a labour of Hercules. As the teacher pointed out in her observations, 'the children are starting to see it as their own.' Good leading of worship opens up the possibility of partnership with the pupils.

Have A Structure
The structure brought two key points of worship into play. Firstly, it allowed children to grow in security. They could relax because they knew what was happening. Secondly, it allowed them to 'grow up.' Children grew into the roles because they perceived the structure of the worship allowed them to do what they needed to do rather than trying to anticipate what was coming next.

Do Not Be Swayed By Novelty
Even from my simple observations it seems clear to me that the people who are better at sitting still and being quiet are children not adults. As G K Chesterton pointed out 'because children have a bounding vitality, because they are in spirit fierce and free, therefore they want things repeated and unchanged.'

Less is More
For me there has been a steep learning curve in this experiment. By far the most significant eye opener has been on the use of the Bible. I have been astounded by the way the children could remember the details of St Columba and the Bible verses, yet no huge amount of information was given to them. Bible passages that are too large are simply too much.

Trust Them With the Bible

In class worship no attempt was made to explain the readings. I am convinced that this is a way forward in such a context. If I, or anybody else, had tried to 'explain away' what was read the children would have tried hard to remember the explanation rather than the story. In this respect we need to adopt the wisdom of the Desert Fathers.

> One day some of the brethren came to see Abba Anthony, and among them was Abba Joseph. Wishing to test them the old man mentioned a text from Scripture and starting with the youngest he asked them what it meant. Each explained it as best he could. But to each one the old man said, 'you have not yet found the answer.' Last of all he said to Abba Joseph, 'and what do you think the text means?' He replied, 'I do not know.' Then Abba Anthony said, 'Abba Joseph has found the way, for he said; I do not know.'[14]

If it is true that 'the spirit blows where it wills' and 'the word of God is sharper than any two-edged sword' then who am I to chase the wind or blunt the blade? Clearly this is not to say that you cannot have any understanding of a biblical text. However, as Kallistos Ware points out, a God 'whom we claim to understand exhaustively through the resources of our reasoning brain turns out to be no more than an idol.'[15]

Practise

Obvious really, but we do so little of it in our adult worship that it is very easy to forget it with our children. Practising and encouraging each other leads to standards. Standards lead to quality and the kind of familiarity that opens up the possibility of our hearts and minds being open to God not what happens next.

Rotate

It is easy for a child to lead for half a term and another child to be in charge of reading for half a term, for another child to do the prayers for half a term. After the end of half a term the roles can switch.

Music

It *must*, I will say that again, it *must* be there. Music is the language of the soul. Music does something that words alone cannot.

On one Thursday, at our school worship in church, I taught the children to sing the Taizé Chant, *O Lord, hear my prayer*. The following Thursday the worship was in school because it was Harvest and we like to get plenty of parents in as well. The worship was in the school hall which has three entrances. At one entrance I started Y6 and Y5 singing the chant. They then walked into the hall singing the chant as they found their places. As they were doing this I started Y3 and Y4 singing in time with Y5 and Y6 and they came into the hall to find their places. As they were doing so the Headteacher led in Y1 and Y2 and Reception who simply joined in with the singing and found their places. We continued for a while until the parents got the message and joined in. The following Tuesday we used the chant in class. All this worked and I cannot even sing!

We are currently exploring the possibility of building a block of common material between church and school that can be sung easily by adults and children alike in any context at All Saints. I would strongly urge all churches with a school to consider doing this.

I took some advice on the teaching of singing and was given the following:[16]

1 When teaching children to sing give them the whole amount in one go not in bits. They seem to enjoy taking a full song or a full tune that can settle into their minds for future reference.

2 If possible try and encourage the children to make a picture in their minds of the song they are singing.

3 Have a go. Most singing falls by the wayside in our country simply because we are too embarrassed to have a go.

Make Blocks
As a result of the experiences outlined above and a discussion with the head on the nature of learning, I feel it is important that the learning of liturgical and musical material should be done in blocks. New liturgical responses and new music should be learned over periods of at least half a term to create familiarity and memory.

Conclusion

'A "knapsack" of liturgical and devotional material for individual use needs to be identified.'[17] What has emerged in our experiment is that we are helping children to discover a knapsack of material that will be available to them in their entire journey through life.

The Lectionary 6

The selection of Scripture, even for the simplest of occasions, can be problematic. In an average class a school year will have seen, for various children, joy at the birth of siblings, special family occasions, divorce, death, new academic challenge, a move to a new house.

In short there will be everything that can happen to an adult in the space of a year. Readings must allow for life. At the same time they must be true to the biblical narrative without passages being taken out of context. Does the exhortation, 'You who fear the Lord, praise him!' (Psalm 22.23) make sense unless you consider the opening verse of the psalm, 'My God, my God, why have you forsaken me?'

I suggest that the following principles must underpin the creation of an appropriate lectionary. These are not in any order of priority.

- Faithfulness to the church's year
- Faithfulness to Scripture
- Less is more
- Cultural context
- The opportunity for teaching in RE
- Translation and accessibility
- The skill of the listener
- The skill of the reader
- Where possible try and use self-contained passages and stories

The following sample is from a lectionary built around Year B, All Saints 2002 to Ash Wednesday 2003. The lectionary states the main Thursday reading and the suggested *lectio divina* for class worship. It takes into account some of the thematic material from *New Patterns for Worship* (November 2002) and seeks to demonstrate how an appropriate lectionary, faithful to church *and* locality, can be put together.

The prologue to this lectionary is Bible Sunday. This can cause some difficulties because of half-term, but if we take the principle of marking out

23

a day for the Bible we could mark out a week for the Bible in school in which we teach pupils and staff the Christian new year is about to start. We can explain that the main part of the Bible to be read is the Gospel of St Mark and use prayer and songs to thank God for the Bible. Schools and churches can be as creative with this week as they wish.

The key to the readings is:

1 Where possible they will mirror the readings from the Sunday before, that is, the start of the Christian week not the week to come.

2 Two readings are given. The main reading to be used on a Thursday and the shorter *lectio divina* reading for use in class worship or at any other time during the school week.

3 Explanatory footnotes are given where the lectionary departs from these simple guidelines.

4 Topics are suggestions of what may be usefully pursued in worship. The three considerations are (a) the church's year; (b) the needs of the pupils in terms of Christian education; (c) issues that might be around in the life of the school—group commemoration, celebration, sadness and so on.

Conclusions

It is only when you begin to write a lectionary that a number of missiological truths confront you. I suspect that these truths are as applicable to adults as to children.

• It is impossible to do justice to the richness and breadth of the Bible in an academic year. The aim should be to 'leave an impression' and plant seeds.

• Our culture has 'moved' far more than many of us realize. We are beginning to discover, even in the 'traditional' North of England, that many children entering school do not know the Nativity. There may come a point when we have to simplify further what has been created above.

• 1600 years of Western culture is about to slip into a black hole. Sound dramatic? How can you understand Western art, literature, science and mathematics unless you know the Nativity, the Crucifixion, Resurrection, conversion of St Paul etc. Not to mention calendar, institutions, and constitution.

- A lectionary 'needs to be seen as serious—as one of the most profound expressions of Christian mission.'[18] For children to hear the Judaeo-Christian story is to engage with a different world and to open up the possibility of choice. There is a different way of living.

- We should not be afraid of the 'strangeness' or the 'extremities' of the Bible. They may not match our ideals of how the world should be, but they can be incredibly contemporary in terms of how the world is. The primary question of the pilgrim is not, How would I like life to be? but, Where is God in all this?

DATE	SEASON	READINGS	TOPIC/ TALK/ ACTIVITY
1st Nov	All Saints	Matthew 5.1–12[1] Matthew 5.1, 2	Listening to Jesus
7th	Bible Week (T/f'd from w/c 27th Oct because of All Saints)	Mark 1.9–12[2] Hebrews 4.12a[3]	Who was Mark?
14th	Ordinary Time	Psalm 149.1–5 Psalm 149.1	Learn a new song or refresh an Advent song
21st	Ordinary Time	Psalm 89.1–4 Psalm 89.20	As above
28th	Advent 1[4]	Mark 13.24–28 Mark 13.26	What does Son of Man mean? God is bigger than the world.
5th Dec	Advent 2	Mark 1.1–8 Mark 1.6	What funny characters God uses. What does the Holy Spirit look like?
12th	Advent 3	John 1.6–8 John 1.8	What does it mean to speak about Jesus? Darkness and light in our world.[5]
19th	Advent 4	Luke 1.26–35 Luke 1.28	God sends messengers. God chooses who to use. The Holy Spirit in action again.
	CHRISTMAS	HOLIDAYS	

DATE	SEASON	READINGS	TOPIC/ TALK/ ACTIVITY
9th Jan	EPIPHANY[6]	Matthew 2.1–12 Matthew 2.11	The Wise men came at Christmas. How old was Jesus? A great Adventure. Not everyone likes Jesus.
16th	Epiphany 1	Mark 1.4–11 Mark 1.10	Jesus gets baptized—we get baptized. Water as a sign of life. The importance of physical things in faith. *ie* Jesus gets dunked not sprinkled.
23rd	Ordinary Time[7]	Gen 6.5–8, 14, 17–22 Gen 6.9	Try to have the story read as a meditation. Pupils eyes closed. Concentrate on breathing and practise listening skills. Simply let them get the story.
30th	Ordinary Time	Gen 7.11, 14–16, 22 Gen 7.15	As above.

6th Feb	CANDLEMAS[8]	Either Luke 2.25–33
		or Luke 2.36–38
		One of: Luke 2.32
		          Luke 2.37
		          Luke 2.38
			Who is this Jesus? What did Jesus come to do?

13th	Ordinary Time	Gen 8.6–13 Gen 8.13	As Jan 23rd.
20th	Ordinary Time	Gen 9.8–13 Gen 9.13	As Jan 23rd.
27th	Half Term		
5th Mar (Wed)	ASH WEDNESDAY	Matthew 6.16–18 Matthew 6.17	No talk–simply imposition of ashes.[9] You can give up things as well as buy them.

A lectionary covering the whole of the year can be found on the Grove web site www.grovebooks.co.uk.

Further Thoughts 7

The issues raised in the comments on building cohesive Christian worship in Church schools need to be developed much further.

In particular the following areas strike me as needing a great deal of thinking through and clear communication between liturgists and educationalists.

How do people learn? My understanding is that educationalists have several views on development. Do the principles they expound apply to adult learning in terms of liturgical formation? Are children liturgically formed differently from adults? 'When I was a child I thought like a child...' (1 Cor 13.11).

What is the role of 'story' in education and liturgy? How do the messages given in the words and actions of our worship and education processes create opportunity for Christ-like growth? How is the imagination awakened and sustained with the Christian meta-narrative?

What is the purpose of 'Time'? Liturgical time is or ought to feel different from normal time. What is the role or function of time in education? Are there any lessons to be learnt by either side? Is it possible to create a community that has a rhythm and life of time that is resistant to the pressures bearing in on us from the world around?

The Global World. Westnocentricity (I cannot think of a better word, other than arrogance) is a major problem. How is our view of the world shaped by our geographical location? Do we push our children too hard in our Western culture in a drive to stay top of the pile? There is a lot of talk about needing more prayerful and reflective worship but Western liturgy is linear unlike Byzantine or Oriental Orthodox worship which is much more cyclical and rhythmic. Given an emphasis in *Common Worship* on such sources as the Liturgy of St Basil, what do we have to say about styles of reflective worship and learning that may be not just renewing but also prophetic in a world that seems to more and more reflect the values of McDonalds rather than of Christ? Do Western liturgy and educational processes reflect and reinforce Western values, rendering themselves incapable of challenging the cultural *status quo*?

Notes

1   C Brown, *The Death of Christian Britain* (London: Routledge, 2001) p 7.
2   *op cit*, p 14. It is, of course, debatable at what time Britain was ever a 'Christian' nation.
3   J Fenwick and B Spinks, *Worship in Transition* (Edinburgh: T & T Clark, 1995) p 105.
4   I am grateful for the time given by John Hall to discuss this issue.
5   A Hickford, *Essential Youth: Why Your Church Needs Young People* (Eastbourne: Kingsway, 1998) p 27.
6   There is a danger of being thought simplistic here but the examples serve to make a point.
7   *On the Way* (GS Misc 444, London: CHP, 1995) p 62, referring to sacramental celebration.
8   Diocese of Blackburn Clergy Conference, College Ripon St John, September 2000.
9   R Warren, *Building Missionary Congregations* (London: Church House Publishing, 1995) p 7.
10 See T Ware, *The Orthodox Church* (London: Penguin, 1997) pp 281 and 288.
11 Every school is required by law to have a plan, agreed by the Governing Body, as to how it is going to develop its life and work. In Church schools RE and Collective Worship should be part of this.
12 R Williams, *Lost Icons: Reflections of Cultural Bereavement* (Edinburgh: T & T Clark, 2000) p 12.
13 The monastic practice whereby a phrase, sentence or verse of Scripture is taken and meditated upon throughout the day.
14 Quoted in K Ware, *The Orthodox Way* (Oxford: Mowbray, 1979) p 12.
15 *Ibid* p 13.
16 This advice is thanks to Wendy Slater who trained as a singer at the Royal Northern College of Music.
17 *On the Way*, p 3.
18 Michael Vasey (and others) *Introducing the New Lectionary*, Grove Worship 141, p 6.

Notes on the Lectionary

1   This is a very full reading. However, it is an exception that tests the rule of less is more. The report *On the Way* recommends five central texts for liturgical focus and formation, one of which is the Beatitudes. *ibid*, p 45.
2   This is not the recommended reading for Bible Sunday. However, as the purpose of this week is to introduce to pupils the idea that the church will concentrate mainly on one of the gospels for the coming 12 months, some compromise must be made to avoid confusion.
3   Where good reason may be found, such as identifying a key biblical verse, the *lectio divina* is taken from another source other than the main reading. Otherwise it is taken from the main reading so as to reinforce the text.
4   Advent is kept as strictly as possible. Some would argue that you need to give pupils the whole Christmas story before the end of term or it will be lost once the New Year starts. I am not persuaded by this argument for two reasons. First, there is a good deal of Christmas 'around' in school, such as nativity services, for children not to miss out. Secondly, the strong emphasis on Epiphany in *Common Worship* gives us a natural vehicle for exploring the nature of the Christian story taking place in 'time.' It allows us to physically mark out an alternative to our culture of, 'see it, buy it, consume it, move on.' The truth works through time not consumer demand.
5   Anyone who is unsure about how to deal with some of the 'weightier' issues in our culture should spend some time watching the excellent BBC *Newsround* programme aimed at dealing with current affairs for the young.
6   Feast Days are an opportunity to keep Year 6 in church with the adults so they can 'see' the Communion service as per chapter 3.
7   Yes! I know that strictly speaking this is not Ordinary Time. However, some compromise must be made. The liturgical year from Advent to Ascension is so rich and intense it is difficult to find useful space. Here I have sacrificed two of the Sundays of Epiphany in order to allow the children to hear one of the great Old Testament stories. The story of a flood is of course one of the great foundational myths of humanity and by placing it in this context, that is, after the Baptism of Christ with Feast of Candlemas in the middle I am attempting to give the children the Christological key by which to understand the story, the Baptism of Christ and their own baptism. For practical purposes it will be necessary to type out the readings over these weeks so that they can be read fluently.
8   The 'resurrection' of Candlemas in *Common Worship* as a major feast is a great gift to Church schools. Children identify with children and what happens to them. They know that, like Jesus, they will one day become that strange thing known as an adult and, again like the infant Jesus, they are 'innocent' as to what life will hold for them.
9   We have found the most effective way of doing this is to appoint a child from each class. At the time for the imposition of ashes the staff and the appointed children come forward to receive the ashes. Having had them placed on their foreheads the children are then given a small saucer containing ashes. They go back to where their class is sat and put ashes on everybody else. This works with minimum teacher supervision. The 'talk' comes simply in the explanation of what is taking place.